THE ULTIMATE GUIDE TO SOCIAL MEDIA INFLUENCER MARKETING

Elevated Influencer Series

Trent Goodbaudy

ElevatedInfluencer.com

*Dedicated to those who wish
to have financial freedom and an enjoyable life in
service to others via social media.*

*Deuteronomy 8:18 "But thou shalt remember the
Lord thy God: for it is he that giveth thee power to
get wealth, that he may establish his covenant which
he sware unto thy fathers, as it is this day."*

CONTENTS

Forward

Welcome to the world of social media influence, where a few keystrokes and a carefully crafted post can have the power to reach millions of people around the globe. Social media has revolutionized the way we communicate, and with it, the way we market products and services.

In this book, we aim to provide you with a comprehensive guide to navigating the exciting and dynamic world of social media influencer marketing. Our team at Elevated Influencer has decades of combined experience in the industry, and we've seen firsthand the power of influence in action. We hope to share our knowledge and expertise with you, so that you too can find success in this burgeoning field.

Whether you're an aspiring social media influencer just starting out, or an experienced pro looking to take your brand to the next level, this book has something for you. From creating compelling content to building your brand and managing your finances, we've got you covered. We'll help you navigate the ever-changing landscape of social media, and provide you with the tools and strategies you need to succeed.

So sit back, grab a latte, and get ready to learn. We're excited to be your guides on this journey to social media influence.

Best regards, The Elevated Influencer Team

INTRODUCTION

The Importance of Social Media Influencers in Today's Digital Age

Let's face it, in today's digital age, social media is king. From TikTok dance challenges to Instagram filters that make us look like we're living our best lives, it's no wonder that social media influencers have become a powerful force in the marketing world.

Gone are the days of relying solely on billboards and TV commercials to get your brand in front of people. Now, all you need is a catchy hashtag and a few hundred thousand followers to become a social media influencer. Okay, it may not be that easy, but you get the point.

Influencer marketing has taken the marketing world by storm, and for good reason. When you partner with a social media influencer, you have the ability to tap into their loyal following and promote your product or service in a way that feels authentic and relatable. Plus, who doesn't love seeing their favorite influencer raving about a product they love?

But it's not just brands that are benefiting from the rise of social media influencers. Influencers themselves have become highly sought after by various industries, from beauty to gaming. As an influencer, you have the power to shape trends and influence consumer behavior in your niche. And let's be real, who doesn't want to be able to do that?

So, in this book, we're going to help you build your personal brand identity as a social media influencer. By developing a strong personal brand, you'll be able to attract and retain a loyal audience and establish yourself as an authority in your niche. Let's get started and turn you into the next big thing in the social media world!

What it Means to be a Successful Social Media Influencer

Now that we've established the importance of social media influencers, let's talk about what it means to be a successful one. Success in the context of social media influence can be defined in many ways, but at its core, it means having a strong following and the ability to influence your audience.

So, what are the characteristics of a successful social media influencer? Well, for starters, they're relatable. Nobody wants to follow someone who seems untouchable or unattainable. Successful influencers connect with their audience on a personal level, whether it's through sharing their daily struggles or their favorite ice cream flavor.

They're also authentic. Authenticity is key in the world of social media, where people are bombarded with sponsored content and #ads on a daily basis. Successful influencers know how to seamlessly weave branded content into their feed without sacrificing their personal brand or losing the trust of their followers.

Another characteristic of successful social media influencers is consistency. You can't build a following overnight, and it takes consistent effort to maintain it. Successful influencers post regularly and engage with their audience on a consistent basis, whether it's through Instagram Stories or TikTok duets.

And of course, successful influencers have a niche. Whether it's beauty, fitness, or even just being a relatable meme queen, successful influencers have a specific niche that they dominate. They know their audience and cater their content to their interests and needs.

But being a successful influencer isn't all about having the perfect feed or the most followers. It's also about being a positive influence on your audience. Successful influencers use their platform to spread positivity and make a difference in the world, whether it's through charity work or spreading awareness about important issues.

In conclusion, being a successful social media influencer is about more than just having a large following. It's about being relatable, authentic, consistent, having a niche, and using your platform for good. So go forth and conquer the social media world, one relatable post at a time!

Potential Benefits of Being a Successful Social Media Influencer

Okay, so we've talked about what it takes to be a successful social media influencer. But what are the potential benefits of achieving this level of success? Let's dive in.

First off, there's the potential for financial gain and brand partnerships. Let's be real, who wouldn't want to get paid to post pictures of themselves sipping a latte or trying out the latest beauty product? Successful influencers have the potential to make a pretty penny from brand partnerships and sponsored content, which can turn their social media hobby into a full-fledged career. Plus, you'll finally be able to afford those trendy avocado toasts that you've been eyeing.

Another benefit of being a successful social media influencer is the ability to impact and inspire others. When you have a large following, you have the ability to spread positivity and make a difference in the world. From sharing motivational quotes to raising awareness about important issues, successful influencers have a platform to inspire change and make a difference. And who doesn't want to be a source of inspiration for others?

And let's not forget about the opportunity to create a personal brand and build a following. As a successful influencer, you have the ability to create a unique personal brand and build a following that is loyal and engaged. Plus, you get to be your own boss and call the shots on what kind of content you create. Want to start a trend of wearing mismatched socks? Go for it, influencer!

But the benefits of being a successful social media influencer go beyond just financial gain and personal branding. You also get to be a part of a larger community of influencers who are passionate about the same things as you. You'll have the opportunity to collaborate with other influencers, attend events, and make connections that can benefit you both personally and professionally.

So, the potential benefits of being a successful social media influencer include financial gain, the ability to impact and inspire others, the opportunity to create a personal brand and build a following, and being a part of a larger community. And let's be real, who wouldn't want to have all of that in their life?

DEFINING YOUR NICHE

Now that you know what it looks like to be a successful social media influencer, it's time to define your niche. But what exactly does that mean? Simply put, your niche is your area of expertise or the topics that you specialize in. So, how do you define your niche? Let's find out.

Identifying Your Strengths and Interests

First and foremost, you need to assess your skills, talents, and passions. What are you good at? What do you enjoy doing? What could you talk about for hours on end? These are all important questions to ask yourself when defining your niche. And let's be real, nobody wants to spend their time creating content about something they hate. Unless that something is kale. Seriously, who likes kale?

Once you've identified your strengths and interests, it's time to analyze your existing content and audience engagement. What types of posts have performed well in the past? What topics have your followers shown the most interest in? And most importantly, what kind of content aligns with your personal brand and your niche? It's important to stay true to yourself and your interests, otherwise you'll end up feeling like a sellout. And nobody wants to be that person.

Defining your niche is all about identifying your strengths and interests and analyzing your existing content and audience engagement. And remember, stay true to yourself and your brand. Unless, of course, you're a fan of kale. In that case, it's time to reevaluate your life choices.

Finding Your Unique Selling Point

Now that you've identified your niche, it's time to find your unique selling point. In other words, what sets you apart from all the other influencers in your niche? What makes you special? Don't worry, it's not just your collection of cat socks.

To find your unique selling point, you need to identify your point of differentiation. What makes you stand out in your niche? Is it your knowledge and expertise? Your sparkling personality? Or is it the fact that you can juggle while riding a unicycle? (Okay, maybe not that last one.) Whatever it is, it's important to leverage it to create compelling content that will resonate with your audience.

But here's the thing: everyone has a unique perspective and story to tell. You just need to find yours. Maybe you're a vegan who loves to travel and has a passion for sustainable fashion. Or maybe you're a fitness enthusiast who also happens to be a parent. Whatever your story may be, use it to your advantage. Share your experiences, your struggles, and your successes. After all, authenticity is key in the world of social media influence. Just be sure to keep it PG-13.

Finding your unique selling point is all about identifying your point of differentiation and leveraging your unique perspective and story to create compelling content. And remember, everyone has a story to tell. Even if yours involves cat socks.

Extra Credit

Your unique selling proposition (USP) is what sets you apart from others in your industry or niche. It's what makes you unique and valuable, and it's what your audience will remember you for.

To reach your unique selling proposition, start by asking yourself what makes you different from everyone else. What sets you apart? What do you do better than anyone else? What do you offer that no one else does?

Think about your strengths and weaknesses, your passions, and your unique perspective. What do you bring to the table that no one else can?

Once you have a clear understanding of your USP, make sure to emphasize it in everything you do. Make it the focus of your content, your branding, and your messaging. Let your audience know why you're different and why they should choose you over others in your industry.

It's important to remember that your USP isn't something that you can fake or manufacture. It's something that's unique to you and comes naturally. It's what sets you apart and makes you stand out, and it's what will ultimately drive your success as an influencer.

So, don't be afraid to be yourself and embrace what makes you unique. Your USP is what will help you rise above the competition and achieve your goals as an influencer. And who knows? Your USP may just be the key to your success and the thing that sets you on the path to becoming the next big thing in your industry!

Targeting Your Audience

Now that you've found your niche and your unique selling point, it's time to target your audience. And no, that doesn't mean throwing tomatoes at random people on the street. It means defining your target audience and creating content that resonates with them.

So, who is your target audience? Well, it depends on your niche and your unique selling point. Are you targeting millennials who love avocado toast and Instagram filters? Or are you targeting baby boomers who prefer a good book and a cup of tea? It's important to define your audience and their characteristics so that you can create content that speaks directly to them. Otherwise, you'll end up like that uncle who tries to be cool by using outdated slang. Trust us, nobody wants to be that uncle.

Once you've defined your target audience, it's time to develop content that resonates with them. This means creating posts, videos, and stories that align with their interests, values, and needs. And let's be real, nobody wants to see a post about the benefits of kale if they're a die-hard meat lover. So, do your research, ask questions, and most importantly, listen to your audience. And if all else fails, just post pictures of cute animals. Who doesn't love a good puppy pic?

Remember: targeting your audience is all about defining your target audience and creating content that resonates with them, be authentic, be relatable, and for the love of all that is good, avoid outdated slang.

BUILDING YOUR BRAND

Creating a Strong and Consistent Brand Image

Now that you've found your niche and your target audience, it's time to build your brand. And no, that doesn't mean you have to start wearing a cowboy hat and boots to appeal to your audience if you're not from Texas. It means defining your brand identity and personality and establishing a consistent visual style and aesthetic.

So, who are you as a brand? Are you sassy and sarcastic? Or are you sweet and wholesome? It's important to define your brand identity and personality so that you can create content that aligns with your brand values. Otherwise, you'll end up like that person who changes their personality to fit in with different groups. And let's be real, nobody likes a fake.

Once you've defined your brand identity and personality, it's time to establish a consistent visual style and aesthetic. This means using the same colors, fonts, and design elements across all of your social media platforms. And no, that doesn't mean you have to use the same filter on every single photo. It means creating a cohesive look and feel that reflects your brand personality.

Consistency is key. You don't want to confuse your audience by using one aesthetic on Instagram and a completely different one on TikTok. That's like wearing a business suit to the beach. It just doesn't make sense.

Building your brand is all about creating a strong and consistent brand image that aligns with your brand identity and personality. And remember, be authentic, be consistent, and for the love of all that is good, avoid being a fake, and wearing a business suit to the beach.

Developing a Content Strategy

Now that you have a strong brand image, it's time to develop a content strategy. This means identifying the type of content that resonates with your audience and planning and scheduling content to ensure consistency.

First and foremost, you need to know what your audience likes. And no, that doesn't mean stalking their Instagram profiles to see what they had for breakfast. It means identifying the type of content that resonates with them. Are they into tutorials, funny memes, or inspirational quotes? Once you know what they like, you can tailor your content to their interests. And if you're really stuck, just go with cat videos. Everyone loves cat videos.

Next, you need to plan and schedule your content to ensure consistency. And no, that doesn't mean posting every hour on the hour. It means creating a content calendar and sticking to it. This will help you stay organized and ensure that you're posting regularly. Plus, it will give you something to blame when you accidentally forget to post that one day. "Oh, sorry, guys. My content calendar was off. I'll make it up to you with more cat videos."

Developing a content strategy is all about identifying the type of content that resonates with your audience and planning and scheduling content to ensure consistency. And remember, when in doubt, just post cat videos.

Creating and scheduling content is a crucial part of any influencer's strategy. Without a plan in place, it can be easy to fall behind and miss opportunities to connect with your audience. In this article, we'll go over the steps you can take to create a content calendar and effectively promote your content.

Extra Credit

Creating, Scheduling, and Organizing Content

Step 1: Define Your Goals and Audience Before you start creating content, it's essential to define your goals and audience. What message do you want to convey, and who are you trying to reach? This will help you tailor your content to your audience's interests and make sure that it's relevant and engaging.

Step 2: Brainstorm Content Ideas Once you've defined your goals and audience, it's time to brainstorm content ideas. Think about what topics or themes would be relevant and interesting to your followers. Consider the type of content that you want to create, such as blog posts, videos, or social media posts.

Step 3: Create a Content Calendar A content calendar is a schedule of when you plan to create and publish your content. It can be as simple or as detailed as you'd like, but the most important thing is to have a plan in place. You can use a spreadsheet, online tool, or even a physical planner to organize your content and schedule.

Step 4: Schedule Your Content Once you've created your content calendar, it's time to start scheduling your content. You can use social media scheduling tools like Hootsuite or Buffer to automate your posts and make sure that they go out at the right time.

Step 5: Promote Your Content Promoting your content is just as important as creating it. Use social media platforms, email marketing, and other channels to share your content with your audience. You can also collaborate with other influencers or brands to expand your reach and connect with new followers.

In conclusion, creating and scheduling content is a crucial part of any influencer's strategy. By defining your goals and audience, brainstorming content ideas, creating a content calendar, scheduling your content, and promoting it effectively, you can connect with your audience and build a successful brand as an influencer.

Establishing Your Voice and Tone

In addition to having a strong brand image and content strategy, it's important to establish your voice and tone. This means developing a distinctive tone and voice for your content and ensuring that it aligns with your brand identity and target audience.

Your tone and voice are what set you apart from other influencers. They give your content personality and make it stand out. Are you funny? Serious? Witty? Sarcastic? It's important to know what your tone is so that you can keep it consistent across all of your content. And if you're not sure what your tone is, just ask yourself: "What would Beyoncé do?"

In addition to having a distinctive tone and voice, it's important to make sure that it aligns with your brand identity and target audience. If your target audience is young and hip, you might want to use more casual language and slang. If your brand identity is more serious, you might want to use more professional language. And if you're not sure what your brand identity or target audience is, just ask yourself: "What would Beyoncé do?"

Establishing your voice and tone is all about developing a distinctive tone and voice for your content and ensuring that it aligns with your brand identity and target audience. And if you're ever in doubt, just remember to ask yourself: "What would Beyoncé do?"

GROWING YOUR FOLLOWING

Building an Engaged Community

Now that you've established your brand and content strategy, it's time to build an engaged community. You want to make sure that your followers are not just random bots or people who accidentally followed you while scrolling through their feed at 3am. You want to build a community of real people who are interested in your content and are willing to engage with you.

Engagement is key! You need to engage with your audience through comments, direct messages, and other channels. This means responding to comments and messages, thanking your followers for their support, and asking for their input and feedback. And if you're ever in doubt, just remember what your mom always told you: "Treat others the way you want to be treated." That's right, it's time to use those manners you learned in kindergarten.

Creating a sense of community is also important. You want to encourage conversations and interactions among your followers. This means asking questions, creating polls, and starting discussions. Think of it like a virtual cocktail party, but with less alcohol and fewer embarrassing dance moves.

Building an engaged community is all about engagement and creating a sense of community among your followers. And if you're ever in doubt about how to engage with your audience, just remember what your mom said and use those manners!

Increasing Your Reach and Visibility

So, you've built an engaged community and now you want to take over the world... or at least expand your reach and visibility. It's time to get strategic!

One of the easiest ways to increase your visibility is by using hashtags and geotags. Think of hashtags as little search engines within social media platforms. They help people find content that they're interested in, and they help your content get discovered by people who are looking for it. And geotags are like a digital GPS that tells people where you are, and where you've been. So, if you're posting pictures of your food adventures, use the geotag to let people know where you found that amazing sushi burrito!

Collaborating with other influencers and brands is also a great way to reach new audiences. Think of it like a crossover episode between your favorite TV shows. You get to team up with other influencers who share your niche or target audience, and create content that will appeal to both of your followers. It's a win-win situation!

Just remember, when it comes to increasing your reach and visibility, it's all about getting strategic with your hashtags, geotags, and collaborations. And who knows, maybe one day you'll be trending on Insta like a certain fluffy cat that we all know and love.

Utilizing Different Social Media Platforms Effectively

When you think about it, social media is like a buffet - there's something for everyone! But not all platforms are created equal, and it's important to choose the ones that will give you the most bang for your buck (or in this case, the most likes for your posts).

First things first, identify which platforms your target audience is most active on. Are they Insta-obsessed? TikTok fiends? Or are they more of a LinkedIn crowd? Once you've nailed that down, it's time to develop platform-specific content and strategies that will make your content shine brighter than a diamond-encrusted unicorn.

For example, if you're a foodie looking to showcase your culinary creations, Instagram is your bread and butter (pun intended). Take high-quality photos of your dishes and post them with mouth-watering captions and hashtags like #foodporn and #delicious. If you're a fitness enthusiast, consider creating short workout videos on TikTok and using trendy hashtags like #fitspo and #getfit.

The possibilities are endless, but don't spread yourself too thin by trying to conquer every platform at once. Choose a few that align with your brand and really master them before moving on to others. Remember, it's quality over quantity when it comes to social media!

COLLABORATING WITH BRANDS

Identifying Potential Brand Partnerships

Alright, let's get to the good stuff – making that money, honey! But before you start collaborating with every brand under the sun, it's important to identify your ideal brand partners. Who do you want to work with, and why?

Think about your niche and your target audience. Are there any brands that align with your values and your content? Do you already use and love any products or services that you could naturally incorporate into your posts?

Once you've identified some potential brand partners, do your research. Check out their existing partnerships and see if there are any opportunities for you to collaborate. But please, for the love of all that is holy, don't just blindly send out cold emails to every brand you come across. Nobody likes a spammer.

Instead, approach potential brand partners strategically and show them why you're the perfect fit for their brand. And if all else fails, just start your own line of branded merch – because who doesn't want to rock a t-shirt with your message?

Approaching Brands and Pitching Collaborations

Approaching brands for collaborations can be a bit nerve-wracking, but it doesn't have to be. After all, they're just companies, not alien life forms trying to invade the planet. Here are some tips to help you craft a winning pitch:

Highlight your unique value proposition: What makes you stand out from the crowd? Is it your witty banter? Your cat's impeccable fashion sense? Your ability to juggle flaming swords? Whatever it is, make sure to include it in your pitch.

Do your research: Make sure to research the brand and their existing partnerships before reaching out. You don't want to pitch a collaboration that's completely irrelevant to their brand or has already been done before.

Be genuine: Building relationships with brands takes time and effort. Don't just pitch and run; engage with them on social media, comment on their posts, and show them that you're genuinely interested in their brand.

Don't be too pushy: Brands receive countless pitches every day, so it's important to be respectful of their time and priorities. Follow up once or twice, but don't spam their inbox or demand an immediate response.

Remember, the key to successful brand collaborations is building relationships and adding value to both parties. So don't be afraid to get creative and have fun with it!

Negotiating and Securing Deals

Now comes the fun part, the money talks! Negotiating and securing brand deals can be a bit daunting, but fear not, we'll make sure you don't end up feeling like a bargain bin influencer.

First things first, you need to understand the different types of brand deals and compensation models available. From paid partnerships and sponsor-ships to gifted products and affiliate marketing, there are many ways to work with brands.

Once you've identified your ideal partnership and compensation model, it's time to put your negotiation skills to the test. Remember, it's not always about getting the most money or free products. You want to make sure the partnership aligns with your values and goals, and that the brand is a good fit for your audience.

So, how do you negotiate like a pro? Well, it's all about finding a win-win situation. You want to offer the brand value and ensure you're compensated fairly for your time and effort.

And if all else fails, remember that you can always go full diva mode and demand a lifetime supply of avocado toast and unicorn frappuccinos. Just kidding, please don't do that.

Extra Credit

I thought that we might like to see an example of how a product deal between a product manufacturer and an elevated social media influencer might play out. Hopefully you will be able to take something away from this dialogue.

Influencer: Hi, thanks for taking the time to talk with me. I'm really excited about the possibility of working with your company.

Manufacturer: We're excited to talk to you too. Your platform has a lot of followers, and we think that our product could be a great fit for your audience.

Influencer: Great! So what are you thinking in terms of a deal?

Manufacturer: We have a few different options we'd like to propose. The first would be a flat fee for a post about our product, and the second would be a commission-based arrangement where you would earn a percentage of sales that result from your promotion.

Influencer: I like the sound of the commission-based option. It's a win-win for both of us, and it gives me an incentive to promote the product as much as possible.

Manufacturer: That's great to hear. We were actually hoping you would be open to that option because we really believe in our product and we think it has the potential to sell really well.

Influencer: I agree. I've done my research on your product and I think it's something my audience would really respond to.

Manufacturer: Well, we're excited to hear that. And we want to sweeten the deal for you even further. In addition to the commission-based arrangement, we'd like to offer you an exclusive discount code that your followers can use to get a discount on our product. And for every sale made using your code, we'll increase your commission rate.

Influencer: That sounds amazing! I'm sure my followers will be thrilled to get a discount, and it's great to know that I'll be earning even more for every sale.

Manufacturer: We're really excited about this partnership, and we think it's going to be a huge success. We're committed to supporting you every step of the way and providing you with all the resources you need to promote our product effectively.

Influencer: Thank you so much! I can't wait to get started. I think this is going to be an amazing opportunity for both of us.

And with that, the influencer and the manufacturer sealed their deal with a handshake, both feeling excited and confident about the partnership ahead. The influencer knew that they had struck an incredible deal and was eager to get to work promoting the product to their audience. Thanks to their creativity and negotiating skills, the influencer came out on top and secured an amazing opportunity to work with a company they truly believed in.

MONETIZING YOUR INFLUENCE

Diversifying Your Revenue Streams

Let's be real, making money is one of the most important parts of being a successful social media influencer. And no, I'm not talking about those paid promotions where you have to pretend like you actually use that slimming tea. I'm talking about real revenue streams that will allow you to make a sustainable income from your influence.

One way to do this is by diversifying your revenue streams. Don't just rely on one source of income, like sponsored posts or brand deals. Instead, consider creating digital products like e-books, courses, or even merchandise. Who wouldn't want a t-shirt with your face on it?

Another option is to get into affiliate marketing. This means you'll earn a commission on any sales made through your unique affiliate link. Just make sure you're promoting products you actually believe in and not just selling out for a quick buck.

The key here is to develop a long-term monetization strategy that aligns with your brand and audience. So, get creative, and don't be afraid to try new things to see what works best for you.

In order to monetize your influence on social media, it's important to have a diversified revenue stream. This means creating multiple ways to make money beyond just sponsored content deals.

As mentioned above, one option is to create and sell digital products like e-books, courses, or even merchandise related to your niche. This can be a great way to leverage your expertise and provide value to your audience while generating revenue.

Another option is to engage in affiliate marketing, which is a type of performance-based marketing where you earn a commission for promoting products or services to your audience. By partnering with brands and promoting their products, you can earn a commission on any resulting sales.

It's important to develop a long-term monetization strategy that aligns with your brand and audience. This means thinking about what products or services would be a natural fit for your audience and niche, and creating a strategy for promoting and selling them. By diversifying your revenue streams and taking a strategic approach to monetization, you can build a sustainable business as a social media influencer.

Creating and Selling Digital Products

So, you've got a bunch of followers, and they trust your opinion on everything from skincare to politics. What's next? Time to create and sell some digital products!

First things first, think about what your audience needs or wants. Maybe they're always asking for your workout routine or your secret to meal prep. Turn that knowledge into an e-book or course and watch the cash roll in.

And hey, if you're not exactly an expert in something, that's okay. Just fake it 'til you make it! Just kidding, don't do that. But seriously, there are plenty of resources out there to help you learn and create valuable content for your followers.

Once you've got your digital product ready, it's time to promote it like there's no tomorrow. Use your social media platforms to show off your product and highlight its benefits. And don't forget to ask your followers to share it with their friends and family.

Selling digital products can be a great way to monetize your influence, but it does take some work. But hey, nothing worth having comes easy, right?

Digital Products:

- Printables: create and sell printables like planners, calendars, worksheets, checklists, and more.
- Stock photos: if you're a photographer or you take great photos, sell them as stock photos.
- Lightroom presets: if you're a skilled photographer, create and sell Lightroom presets.

- Social media templates: create templates for social media posts, stories, and reels that other creators can use.

- E-courses: create and sell courses on topics that you're knowledgeable about, like photography, cooking, fashion, or fitness.

- Webinars: host webinars and sell access to them.

- E-books: write and sell e-books on topics related to your niche.

- Audio content: create and sell audio content like podcasts, audiobooks, or guided meditations.

Physical Products:

- Merchandise: create your own merchandise, like t-shirts, mugs, phone cases, or stickers, that your followers can buy.

- Subscription boxes: create subscription boxes filled with products related to your niche.

- Books: write and publish books related to your niche.

- Beauty or skincare products: if you're in the beauty or skincare niche, create and sell your own products.

- Fitness equipment: if you're in the fitness niche, create and sell your own fitness equipment.

- Fashion items: if you're in the fashion niche, create and sell your own clothing, accessories, or jewelry.

- Artwork: if you're an artist, create and sell your own artwork.

Remember to do your research and make sure that the products you create are high-quality and something that your audience will actually want to buy. Good luck!

Utilizing Affiliate Marketing and Sponsored Content

Affiliate marketing is like recommending your favorite products to your friends, except you get paid for it! You can become an affiliate partner with different companies and earn a commission every time someone buys something using your unique referral link. So, if you've got a great taste in products, this could be a great way to monetize your influence.

Affiliate marketing is a popular way for influencers to monetize their content. Essentially, you promote someone else's product or service and earn a commission for every sale made through your unique affiliate link.

There are a lot of different affiliate programs out there, and it's important to find ones that align with your brand and audience. Some examples of great affiliate opportunities could include:

- Amazon Associates: This program allows you to earn a commission on any qualifying purchases made through your unique affiliate link to Amazon.

- Shopify: If you have an e-commerce or business-focused audience, promoting Shopify's e-commerce platform could be a great opportunity to earn commissions on any new sign-ups.

- Bluehost: If your audience is interested in starting a blog or website, Bluehost offers a popular web hosting service and affiliate program.

- Skillshare: If you create content related to creative skills, promoting Skillshare's online learning platform could be a great fit. They offer a commission for every new user who signs up through your unique affiliate link.

- NordVPN: If you have a tech-focused audience, promoting NordVPN's virtual private network service could be a good opportunity to earn commissions on new sign-ups.

Remember, when it comes to affiliate marketing, it's important to only promote products and services that you truly believe in and that align with your brand and values. Otherwise, your audience may lose trust in you and your recommendations.

Sponsored content is when a brand pays you to create content that promotes their products. This can be anything from a blog post to a social media campaign. The key here is to make sure the sponsored content fits with your brand and your audience, so it doesn't feel like you're just selling out for a quick buck. But hey, if you can get paid for creating content you'd already make for free, that's just smart business.

When it comes to finding great sponsored content opportunities, it's important to look for brands that align with your values and the interests of your audience. This can help ensure that the sponsored content is well-received and doesn't come off as inauthentic or forced.

Some examples of sponsored content opportunities include:

- Sponsored blog posts: You can partner with a brand to create a blog post that features their product or service. For example, a food blogger might partner with a company that sells kitchen gadgets to create a recipe post using their products.

- Sponsored social media posts: Brands will often partner with influencers to create sponsored posts on Instagram, Twitter, or other social media platforms. These posts might feature a product review, a giveaway, or simply a shout-out to the brand.

- Sponsored videos: If you're a YouTuber, you can create sponsored videos that showcase a brand's product or service. For example, a beauty influencer might partner with a skincare company to create a video tutorial using their products.

It's important to make sure that any sponsored content you create is clearly labeled as such, in accordance with FTC guidelines. This can help maintain transparency with your audience and build trust over the long term.

STAYING AUTHENTIC AND ETHICAL

Maintaining Your Integrity and Credibility

As an influencer, it's important to build trust with your audience. You want them to know that what you're promoting is something you truly believe in, and not just something you're doing for the money (although, let's be real, we all gotta eat).

So, how do you build that trust? It starts with transparency and honesty. Don't try to hide sponsored content or pretend that you're not getting paid to promote something. Your audience is smarter than that, and they'll appreciate the honesty.

Another key to maintaining your integrity is to avoid any unethical practices. This includes buying fake followers or engagement. Not only is it dishonest, but it's also not going to help you in the long run. Your audience can spot fake followers from a mile away, and it can actually hurt your credibility.

So, stay true to yourself and your audience. Be honest, be transparent, and don't cut any corners. Your integrity is worth more than any amount of money.

- Disclose sponsored content: Whenever you promote a product or service in exchange for compensation, make sure to disclose it clearly to your audience. This helps maintain transparency and trust with your followers.

- Stay true to your brand: Don't promote products or services that don't align with your brand or values. Your followers are following you for a reason, so it's important to stay true to who you are and what you represent.

- Be mindful of your endorsements: Think carefully before endorsing a product or service. Consider whether it's something you would genuinely use or recommend to your audience.

- Don't buy followers or engagement: It's never a good idea to buy followers or engagement to boost your numbers. Not only is it unethical, but it can also harm your credibility in the long run.

Remember, maintaining authenticity and ethics is crucial for building a strong and sustainable influencer career.

Being Transparent With Your Audience

Look, we get it, you want to make some dough, but don't let that dough come at the cost of your audience's trust. One of the best ways to build a strong and loyal following is to be honest and transparent with them. If you're getting paid to promote something, let them know! Be clear about sponsored content and affiliate links, and make sure your audience knows that you're only recommending products you believe in.

Transparency is key to maintaining your credibility, and without credibility, you're just another influencer shouting into the void. So, be upfront with your audience, and they'll respect you for it. Plus, if you happen to be promoting something totally weird, like a toaster that also doubles as a showerhead, it's better to be upfront about it than have your audience thinking you've gone off the deep end.

And while you're being transparent with your audience, why not also share your values and beliefs? People want to follow someone who stands for something, and by sharing your passions and beliefs, you'll connect with your audience on a deeper level. Just make sure you're not sharing anything too controversial, like your belief that cats are better than dogs (even though we all know they are).

Adhering to Industry Guidelines and Regulations

I know we all like to bend the rules a little bit, but when it comes to influencer marketing, it's important to play by the book. And the book is written by the Federal Trade Commission (FTC). So, before you go promoting that weight loss tea or those fancy new vitamins, make sure you understand the FTC's guidelines for influencer marketing.

And don't forget, each platform has its own set of rules and regulations that you need to follow. I mean, have you ever tried to post a picture of your dog on Instagram only to have it taken down for violating community guidelines? Yeah, it's a real thing. So, just make sure you read up on the rules and don't do anything that could get you banned from your favorite platform.

The Federal Trade Commission (FTC) has specific guidelines that influencers must follow when it comes to sponsored content and affiliate marketing. These guidelines require influencers to clearly disclose any relationships or partnerships they have with brands when promoting their products or services.

Many social media platforms have their own rules and regulations regarding influencer marketing, such as the requirement to use the platform's built-in disclosure tools or to clearly label sponsored posts.

Additionally, different social media platforms have their own rules and regulations when it comes to influencer marketing. For example, Instagram requires influencers to disclose sponsored content using their built-in "Paid Partnership" feature. It's important to do your research and stay up-to-date with any changes or updates to these guidelines to ensure that you're staying ethical and compliant.

It's important for influencers to adhere to these guidelines and regulations not only to avoid legal repercussions, but also to maintain their integrity and credibility with their audience. By being transparent and upfront about sponsored content and affiliate links, influencers can build trust with their followers and maintain a positive reputation within the industry.

MANAGING YOUR BUSINESS

Developing a Business Plan and Setting Goals

Well, well, well... it's time to put on your CEO hat and start thinking about your business plan! Yes, even influencers need to think like business owners. This means setting short-term and long-term goals, and creating a plan that outlines your strategy and tactics.

Think about it this way - you wouldn't set out on a road trip without a map or GPS, right? The same goes for your influencer business. You need a plan to help you reach your destination (success) and to make sure you're on the right path.

So, grab a pen and paper (or a tablet/laptop if you're feeling fancy), and start brainstorming. What are your goals for the next year? Where do you see yourself in five years? And most importantly, how are you going to get there?

Remember, your business plan doesn't have to be set in stone. It's okay to make adjustments and pivot as you go. But having a plan in place will help you stay focused, motivated, and on track to reach your goals.

When it comes to setting goals, it's important to make them specific, measurable, achievable, relevant, and time-bound (SMART). This way, you have a clear idea of what you're working towards and can track your progress along the way.

As for creating a business plan, it's helpful to do some research on your industry and competition, as well as your target audience and potential revenue streams. This will give you a better understanding of the market and how you can position yourself for success. Don't forget to regularly review and update your business plan as needed to reflect changes in your goals and the market.

Here's a sample business plan for a social media influencer:

Business Name: [Your Name] Social Media Influencing

Business Description: As a social media influencer, I use my platform to create content and engage with my followers to promote various products and services. My audience consists of [insert demographic information]. My goal is to increase my reach and engagement, and develop additional income streams through affiliate marketing, sponsored content, and digital product sales.

Marketing Strategy: I will use various social media platforms, including Instagram, YouTube, and TikTok, to create content and engage with my followers. I will also utilize hashtags, geotags, and collaborations with other influencers and brands to increase my visibility and reach new audiences.

Revenue Streams:

Affiliate marketing partnerships with companies in my niche

Sponsored content with brands that align with my values and resonate with my audience

Digital product sales, including e-books, courses, and templates

Expenses:

Production costs, such as camera equipment, editing software, and props

Advertising expenses, such as paid promotions and collaborations

Other general business expenses, such as website hosting, legal fees, and taxes.

Financial Projections:

Projected revenue for the first year: $50,000

Projected expenses for the first year: $20,000

Projected profit for the first year: $30,000

Goals:

- Increase my social media following by 50% in the first year

- Secure 3 new sponsored content partnerships in the first year

- Develop and launch at least 2 digital products within the first year

----

The above business plan can be used to open a bank account and present to potential lenders when seeking a business loan. It provides a clear understanding of the business model, target audience, revenue streams, expenses, and financial projections.

Managing Your Finances and Taxes

Are you making so much money that you don't know what to do with it? Good for you, but you'll want to make sure you're managing your finances and taxes properly so you don't end up with a headache down the line.

First things first, make sure you're tracking all of your income and expenses. You can do this manually or use accounting software to help you out. Just remember, if you're going to do it manually, make sure you're organized or your life is going to be a mess.

Secondly, it's always a good idea to hire an accountant or financial advisor to help you manage your taxes. They'll make sure you're following all the rules and regulations and help you keep as much of your hard-earned money as possible.

Remember, you don't want to end up like some of those celebrities who owe millions of dollars in back taxes. Stay on top of your finances and taxes and you'll be able to enjoy your hard-earned money stress-free.

Here are some tips for managing your finances as a social media influencer:

Keep track of your income and expenses: Make sure to maintain accurate records of all the money coming in and going out of your business. This will help you keep track of your profits and losses, and ensure that you're meeting your financial goals.

Create a budget: Set a budget for your business expenses, such as equipment, travel, and marketing. Stick to it as closely as possible to avoid overspending.

Separate your personal and business finances: Open a separate bank account for your business to keep your personal and business finances separate. This will make it easier to track your expenses and file your taxes.

Consider hiring a financial advisor: If you're not comfortable managing your finances on your own, consider hiring a financial advisor or accountant to help you stay on track.

Save for taxes: As a business owner, you'll be responsible for paying your own taxes. Set aside a portion of your income each month to cover your tax bill at the end of the year.

Remember, managing your finances is an essential part of running a successful business as a social media influencer. By staying organized and keeping track of your income and expenses, you'll be able to make informed decisions about how to grow and scale your business.

Hiring a Team and Delegating Tasks

Look, being an influencer is tough work. You're creating content, building relationships with brands, and monetizing your influence. It can be overwhelming, and that's where a team comes in.

You don't have to do everything by yourself. Identify the tasks that you can delegate to others. Maybe you're not the best at graphic design or video editing. Hire someone who can take that off your plate.

Building a team that complements your strengths and weaknesses is essential. You don't want to hire a bunch of people who are just like you. That would be boring, and it wouldn't help you grow. You need people who can bring different perspectives and skillsets to the table.

So, go ahead and delegate those tasks, build that dream team, and watch your influence skyrocket!

What to look for in a prospective team member and where to find them:

- Look for skills that complement your own: When building a team, it's important to find people who have skills that complement your own. For example, if you're great at creating content but not so great at managing social media, look for someone who excels in social media management.

- Seek out reliable, trustworthy individuals: You want team members who are reliable and trustworthy, so make sure to do your due diligence when considering candidates. Ask for references and check them thoroughly.

- Look for passion and enthusiasm: You want team members who are passionate about what they do and enthusiastic about working with you. Look for candidates who show genuine interest in your brand and what you're trying to achieve.

- Consider cultural fit: Your team members will be spending a lot of time working together, so it's important to find people who fit in with your company culture. Look for candidates who share your values and work ethic.

- Use social media and online platforms: Social media and online platforms like LinkedIn can be great resources for finding prospective team members. You can search for candidates based on their skills and experience, and even post job listings to attract candidates.

- Attend industry events: Industry events and

conferences can be great places to meet and network with potential team members. Attend relevant events in your industry and be sure to bring business cards and a pitch about your brand and what you're looking for in a team member.

Remember, building a great team takes time and effort, but it's well worth it in the long run. By finding the right people to complement your skills and help you grow your brand, you'll be on your way to success.

OVERCOMING CHALLENGES

Dealing With Negativity and Criticism

As a social media influencer, you're bound to get your fair share of haters and trolls. But don't worry, it's all just part of the job! You just need to have a thick skin and a good sense of humor to deal with the negativity and criticism that will inevitably come your way.

To develop resilience and cope with negative feedback, try practicing some self-care techniques like yoga, meditation, or binge-watching Netflix. And don't forget to lean on your support system - whether it's your friends, family, or loyal followers - they'll always have your back.

When it comes to responding to criticism, remember to take a deep breath and resist the urge to fire back with a snarky comment. Instead, try to address the feedback in a constructive and respectful manner. And if all else fails, just remember: haters gonna hate, but influencers gonna influence!

Here are a few more potential challenges that social media

influencers might face:

- Balancing personal life and work demands
- Handling legal issues, such as contracts and intellectual property rights
- Coping with burnout and staying motivated
- Keeping up with changes in technology and platform algorithms
- Managing mental health and the pressure to maintain a public persona

It's important to remember that everyone's journey as a social media influencer will be different, and each person may face unique challenges along the way. However, with a proactive and adaptable mindset, influencers can learn to overcome these obstacles and continue to grow their brand and business.

Adapting to Changes in the Industry

I am sure we can all agree that social media is constantly changing. What's hot one day may be out the next. So, as an influencer, it's important to stay on top of the latest trends and new technologies. But don't worry, you don't need to be a tech genius to do this. Just keep your eyes and ears open and be willing to learn.

And when it comes to embracing change, remember that change can be a good thing. It can give your content and strategy a fresh new look and help you stand out from the crowd. So, don't be afraid to mix things up and try something new. Who knows, you may just start a trend of your own!

Some examples of past changes in the influencer marketing industry that required adaptation:

- Platform algorithm changes: Social media platforms such as Instagram and Facebook often make changes to their algorithms, which can greatly impact the reach and visibility of an influencer's content. In response, influencers must adjust their content and posting strategies to align with the new algorithms.

- Rise of new platforms: With the constant emergence of new social media platforms, influencers must decide whether to expand their presence and create content on these new platforms or stick with their existing ones.

- Increased competition: As the influencer marketing industry grows, so does the competition. Influencers must find new ways to stand out and differentiate themselves from others in their niche.

- Shifting audience interests: The interests and preferences of an influencer's audience can change over time. To remain relevant and engaged, influencers must adapt their content to reflect these changes.

- Legal and regulatory changes: The FTC and other regulatory bodies often update their guidelines and rules for influencer marketing. Influencers must stay informed and adjust their practices to ensure compliance.

Overcoming Burnout and Mental Health Issues

Hey, being an influencer is tough work, and it's easy to get burnt out when you're constantly creating content and engaging with your followers. Here are some tips to help you avoid burnout and keep your mental health in check:

- Take breaks! Don't be afraid to take a day off or a weekend away from social media.

- Practice self-care. This can mean anything from taking a long bath to going for a run or meditating. Do what makes you feel good!

- Connect with other influencers who understand what you're going through. Join online communities or attend events to meet others in your industry.

- Seek professional help if you need it. Mental health is just as important as physical health, and there's no shame in asking for help.

Social media influencers may experience various mental health issues, such as burnout, anxiety, depression, and feelings of inadequacy or imposter syndrome. Additionally, they may also face cyberbullying, negative comments, and even threats, which can take a toll on their mental health. It's essential for influencers to prioritize their mental well-being and seek help when needed.

Remember, taking care of yourself is crucial if you want to

continue to be a successful influencer.

CONCLUSION

The Future of Social Media Influencer Marketing

Well, that's almost it folks! Thanks for tuning in to our wisdom-filled words about the world of social media influencer marketing. But before you go, let's talk about what the future holds for this constantly evolving industry.

First off, let me consult my crystal ball...hmm...it appears that the future of influencer marketing is looking pretty bright. As social media continues to become a more integral part of our daily lives, the demand for authentic and engaging content from influencers will only continue to grow.

But of course, with great demand comes great competition. In order to stay ahead of the curve, influencers will need to constantly innovate and adapt to new technologies and trends. Who knows, maybe we'll even see the rise of hologram influencers in the near future!

But in all seriousness, the potential for growth and innovation in the influencer marketing industry is truly limitless. As long as influencers remain authentic, ethical, and adaptable, the sky's the limit. So go forth, my fellow influencers, and conquer the social media world!

The Potential for Personal and Professional Growth as a Social Media Influencer

Let's talk for a bit about personal and professional growth as a social media influencer!

Being a social media influencer isn't just about getting free products and making sponsored posts, it can also help you develop a plethora of valuable skills. You'll learn how to create compelling content, engage with your audience, and market yourself in a highly competitive industry.

Not only that, but being a social media influencer can also open doors for you beyond the realm of social media. With your newfound skills and experiences, you may find yourself interested in other entrepreneurial ventures, or even using your influence to make a difference in your community.

So don't be afraid to take that leap of faith and pursue your dream of being a social media influencer. Who knows what kind of growth and opportunities lie ahead?

Being a social media influencer can be a challenging but rewarding experience. Not only do you have the potential to grow your following and build your brand, but you can also gain valuable skills and experiences that can benefit you in all areas of your life. From honing your communication and marketing skills to learning how to build a business and manage a team, the opportunities for personal and professional growth are endless.

So, if you're willing to put in the time and effort, the rewards can be truly amazing. Don't be afraid to take risks, embrace change, and always be willing to learn and grow. Who knows where your journey as a social media influencer will take you? The possibilities are endless, and the only limit is your own imagination. So go out there and make your mark on the world!

Final Tips and Advice for Success in the Industry

Now that you've made it to the end of this guide, it's time for some real talk. Here are some key takeaways and lessons learned that can help you succeed in the ever-evolving world of social media influencer marketing:

- Be authentic and true to yourself. Nobody likes a fake influencer, except maybe a bot.

- Always be transparent with your audience. If you're getting paid to promote something, let them know. If you're not getting paid, but just really love that product, also let them know.

- Stay up-to-date with the latest industry trends and changes. Just like how you should stay up-to-date on the latest memes and TikTok challenges.

- Be adaptable and willing to try new things. Like that new vegan kale smoothie that everyone's raving about.

- Take care of your mental health and well-being. After all, you can't be an influencer if you're burnt out and miserable.

And finally, here's some advice for all you aspiring social media influencers out there:

- Find your niche and stick to it like a koala to a eucalyptus tree.

- Collaborate with other influencers, brands, and creatives. Just remember to share the spotlight, like a true influencer unicorn.

- Don't be afraid to make mistakes and learn from them. After all, the best way to learn is through trial and error, just like how you learned not to wear crocs in public.

- Be authentic: It's essential to stay true to yourself and your values while creating content. Your audience can sense when you're being fake or inauthentic, which can negatively impact your reputation.

- Consistency is key: Consistency is crucial when it comes to building your brand and your audience. Be consistent with your content creation, posting schedule, and engagement with your followers.

- Stay up-to-date: Stay informed about the latest trends, updates, and changes in the industry. Keeping up with the latest news and best practices can help you stay ahead of the competition and improve your content strategy.

- Network and collaborate: Building relationships with other influencers, brands, and industry professionals can open up new opportunities for collaborations and sponsorships. Attend events and engage with other influencers in your niche.

- Don't be afraid to try new things: Experimenting with different types of content, platforms, and strategies can help you find what works best for you and your audience. Don't be afraid to take risks and try new things.

- Have fun and enjoy the ride! Remember, social media influencer marketing is all about creating content that inspires and entertains. So, go out there and spread some digital sunshine!

CASE STUDIES

Elevating Ricky

Ricky is a young man who is passionate about health and fitness. Ricky had always been active and loved trying new workouts and healthy recipes. He had a dream of becoming a successful influencer in the health and fitness space, but he knew that the competition was fierce.

To elevate his influencer game and stand out from the competition, Ricky decided to take action. He started by contacting Elevated Influencer LLC who began by assisting him in identifying his unique selling proposition (USP). Ricky realized that his USP was his ability to create customized workout and meal plans for his followers based on their individual needs and goals. He decided to focus on this niche and began creating content that emphasized his personalized approach to health and fitness.

Next, Ricky reached out to other influencers in the health and fitness space and started collaborating with them. He teamed up with a popular fitness YouTuber who had a similar approach to fitness and together, they created a series of workout videos that were a huge hit with their followers.

Ricky also invested in high-quality equipment, including a professional camera and editing software. This helped him to create even better content that was visually stunning and high-quality.

To stay organized and consistent, Ricky created a content calendar. He planned out his posts in advance, ensuring that he was posting regularly and at the best times for his audience. He also made sure to engage with his followers regularly, responding to comments and hosting Q&As to build a loyal following.

As Ricky continued to improve his content and strategy, his following began to grow. He gained more and more followers who loved his personalized approach to health and fitness and his authentic personality. Brands began reaching out to him for sponsored posts and collaborations, and he started to earn a significant income from his influencer work.

Ricky was thrilled with the results of his hard work and dedication. He had transformed his passion for health and fitness into a successful career as an influencer, and he was able to inspire and motivate others along the way. He knew that there was still more to learn and more room to grow, but he was excited for the possibilities that lay ahead.

In the end, Ricky realized that by incorporating these tips into his life, he was able to elevate his influencer game and stand out from the competition. He was able to turn his passion into a successful career, and he learned that there really are no limits other than what you impose on yourself.

Elevating Samantha

Once upon a time, there was a young woman named Samantha who dreamed of becoming a successful influencer. She had always been passionate about fashion and beauty, and she loved sharing her knowledge and insights with others. However, she knew that the competition in the influencer world was fierce, and she wasn't sure how to stand out.

One day, Samantha decided to take action. She started by reaching out to Elevated Influencer LLC who began by assisting her in identifying her unique selling proposition (USP). She realized that her USP was her love for vintage fashion and her ability to style vintage pieces in a modern and trendy way. She decided to focus on this niche and began creating content that emphasized her vintage style.

Next, based on direction from Elevated Influencer LLC, Samantha reached out to other influencers in the vintage fashion space and started collaborating with them. She teamed up with a popular Instagram influencer who had a similar aesthetic and together, they created a series of vintage-inspired photoshoots that were a huge hit with their followers.

Samantha also invested in high-quality equipment, including a professional camera and lighting equipment. This helped her to create even better content that was visually stunning and high-quality.

To stay organized and consistent, Samantha created a content calendar. She planned out her posts in advance, ensuring that she was posting regularly and at the best times for her audience. She also made sure to engage with her followers regularly, responding to comments and hosting Q&As to build a loyal following.

As Samantha continued to improve her content and strategy, her following began to grow. She gained more and more followers who loved her unique vintage style and her authentic personality. Brands began reaching out to her for sponsored posts and collaborations, and she started to earn a significant income from her influencer work.

Samantha was thrilled with the results of her hard work and dedication. She had transformed her passion for vintage fashion into a successful career as an influencer, and she was able to inspire and motivate others along the way. She knew that there was still more to learn and more room to grow, but she was excited for the possibilities that lay ahead.

In the end, Samantha realized that by incorporating these tips into her life, she was able to elevate her influencer game and stand out from the competition. She was able to turn her passion into a successful career, and she knew that the sky was the limit.

A day in the life of a successful social media influencer

I wake up early in the morning, around 6 AM, and check my phone for any important messages or notifications. Then, I hit the gym for an hour or so to get my blood pumping and start the day off on a positive note. After that, I head back home and take a quick shower before sitting down at my desk to begin work.

As a social media influencer, my job requires a lot of planning and strategizing. I spend the first couple of hours of my day responding to emails, checking my social media accounts, and brainstorming ideas for my next post or campaign. I also spend time reviewing my analytics to see which content is performing the best and adjust my strategy accordingly.

Around mid-morning, I usually have a conference call with my team to discuss any ongoing projects or campaigns. This is also a good time for me to brainstorm new ideas with my creative team and plan out any upcoming shoots or collaborations.

In the afternoon, I typically spend a few hours shooting content for my social media accounts. This could involve taking photos, filming videos, or even doing live streams. I'm always looking for new and exciting ways to engage my audience, so I try to be as creative as possible with my content.

Once I've finished shooting, I'll spend some time editing and captioning my content before scheduling it to go live on my various social media platforms. I try to keep a consistent posting schedule, so my followers always know when to expect new content from me.

As the day starts to wind down, I'll usually take some time to engage with my followers by responding to comments, direct messages, and emails. I value my relationship with my audience, so I try to be as active and engaged as possible.

In the evening, I might attend a social event or meeting with potential collaborators. This is a great opportunity for me to network and make new connections in the industry.

Finally, before heading to bed, I'll take some time to plan out my schedule for the next day and review any upcoming campaigns or projects. Being a successful social media influencer requires a lot of hard work and dedication, but I wouldn't have it any other way.

NOW THAT YOU HAVE READ THE BOOK

Please go leave a review on Amazon and then send a screenshot to CONTACT@ELEVATEDINFLUENCER.COM and we will send you a thank you offer or discount!

Visit ELEVATEDINFLUENCER.COM today!